TRUMPLETHINSKIN AND THE WIZARD BONESPURS

FIRST EDITION
Trumplethinskin and the Wizard Bonespurs © 2020 by Martin Treanor
Cover art © 2020 by Martin Treanor
Interior & cover design © 2020 by dprz.net

All Rights Reserved.

This book is a work of fiction. Names, characters, places, and incidents are either a product of the author's imagination or are used fictitiously. Any resemblance to actual events, locales, or persons, living or dead, is entirely coincidental.*

Tiny Hands Press
an imprint of DRPZ Publishing
drpz.net

*except for Trumplethinskin

TRUMPLETHINSKIN AND THE WIZARD BONESPURS

Martin Treanor

DEDICATION

Martin Treanor—for, yes, it is he—would like to thank a whole stack of people: Sal, Sandra, Steve, Marg, Colin, and the Trumplethinskin himself, whose mastery of the spoken word and stable geniusnessness provided the inspiration for these, as Fibber Fox might say: **Tall Tall Tales**.

Martin—for it is indeed he—would also like to thank his wife, daughter, and daughter's partner for their support with the project, and lastly and maybe but maybe not least, Mr. A himself who is just oh so dreamy, OMG, I can't even. . . .
(He made me say that.)

Trumplethinskin was a crotchety chap—with a roly-poly belly, wispy fly-away hair, and a jowly orange face that looked like a pumpkin—who lived in a bigly big house he called *Mangy Logo*, which actually wasn't its real name. Poor old Trumplethinskin, "*didn't do wurds good.*"

Anyway, one bright morning, after many hours of looking at the pictures in his favorite storybook—*Fibber Fox's Tall Tall Tales*—Pencho the House Elf told him that the town criers were telling all the realm about the time—many, many years ago—when a letter arrived from somewhere called Vet Nam, saying that Trumplethinskin had to come to visit.

You see, Trumplethinskin hadn't always been old and crotchety. When he was younger he was fit as a fool, but no less roly-poly—or, in fact, crotchety. And, back then, although others were being sent to Vet Nam, Trumplethinskin didn't want to go. It was a nasty, dangerous place where people fought with each other, and not a single person had a golden toilet.

And, anyway, anything Trumplethinskin didn't like was fake news.

He wanted to stay at home, lie on his bed, eat beautiful chocolate cake, and dream about how—someday—he would be so mega-rich he would have more golden toilets than anyone else in all the realm, and maybe even be the *King of Not Far Far Away Enough*, with his very own throne —a real throne—not just a golden toilet.

He also wanted to stay home so he could play *Grab the Kitty* with Cinderella, Sleeping Beauty, and Snow White (white being Trumplethinskin's most favorite color), even though they didn't want to play with him.

Psst! Sleeping Beauty wasn't really sleeping.

But, as luck would have it, even then, and to his own mind at least, Trumplethinskin was a stable genius. Some people—mostly the stupid hobgoblins called *Magas*—said he was very, very, very intelligent, and he had many, many beautiful, incredible, and beautiful ideas. Like the time, later on, when he started casinos, and magazines, and learning-colleges that would make people know words just as good as him—and they did—before they were all closed down.

Psst! His favorite idea, though, was doing charities—"*Some people will give you their last magic bean,*" he remembered thinking, "*and with loads of other people's magic beans, I can buy a big portrait of myself to hang over my four-poster bed.*"

So, Trumplethinskin had his first beautiful idea: When Daffy Draft—the bossy soldier with the shiny buttoned coat—turned up to take him away, he would pretend that booboos had started growing all over his tootsies . . .

. . . and, like his nose when he told fibs, they had grown large and as red, swollen, and angry as Hennity Bennity's big bulbous head.

And Daffy Draft did come, but didn't believe that Trumplethinskin had booboos on his tootsies.

So, Trumplethinskin went trotting off into Wharton Woods to find the elusive Wizard Bonespurs who had the power to make-believe anything.

Through the trees he went, dodging all sorts of obstacles and transmittable diseases that could be caught from just sleeping around the place until, finally, he arrived at the ramshackle old cabin where the Wizard Bonespurs lived.

Knock, knock, knock—he knocked on the door.

But no one answered.

Knock, knock, knock—he knocked again. Eventually, the door opened and a wizened old man appeared.

"What do you want?" the old man, the Wizard Bonespurs bellowed.

"I need a favor," Trumplethinskin replied. In the years to come, he would ask for many favors from all sorts of strange beings—some who lived in other realms—and only when it made him look good.

"What kind of favor?"

"Daffy Draft says I have to go to Vet Nam. And I don't want to go to Vet Nam. I don't want to go there one tiny little bit." And then he cried, "Wah – wah – wah." He bawled and bawled and bawled.

Trumplethinskin cried a lot because, actually, he really was the bigly biggest baby.

And then he huffed.

(Trumplethinskin huffed a lot too, and complained, and whinged, and generally didn't like anything that wasn't saying good things about him. He also didn't have any friends, except for those he bought with Daddy Trumplethinskin's big bulging bag of magic beans.)

Anyway, as it happened, when the Wizard Bonespurs heard that Trumplethinskin's daddy had a bulging bag of magic beans, he became very interested. He dashed back inside, returned with a roll of parchment, and handed it to Trumplethinskin.

"Take this," the wizard said.

"What is it?"

"It's a magic scroll. It says you actually do have booboos on your tootsies and that they are very, very sore. Show it to Daffy Draft.

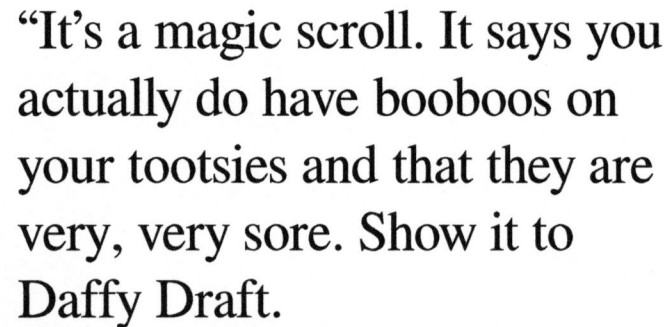

"Tell him how you bought it from me, and mention that your daddy has loads of magic beans. It will make him go away, leave you alone, and find some other poor dope (who doesn't have a rich daddy, and not even a golden toilet) to go in your place."

Well, Trumplethinskin was overjoyed. So much so, he decided he would build a really tall tower in celebration. But that's another story altogether. With a spring in his step—because he really didn't have booboos on his tootsies—he went back to *Mangy Logo*, ordered a shed-load of beautiful chocolate cake, lay down on his bed, and unrolled the parchment.

The page was bare.

There were no *wurds*.

What would he do? The Wizard Bonespurs had sold him a dud.

And then it all became clear to him. The parchment was a big fat lie. There was nothing written on the page because his tootsie booboos weren't actually there—he did have a yellow belly, though, which he liked, almost as much as his flabby orange face.

Anyway, although he was "*as thick as all the short planks in the realm*"—as his teacher, Mr. Fordham used to say—Trumplethinskin also discovered something amazing.

Because, if the Wizard Bonespurs could make-believe a roll of paper good enough to con Daffy Draft into finding some other poor dope to go to Vet Nam instead of Trumplethinskin, then so could Trumplethinskin himself.

From this moment forward, he would spend the rest of his life make-believing everything he did or said, telling nothing but big fat lies, selling duds, and stiffing everyone he came across for their last magic bean . . .

. . . in fact, he vowed to swindle and con all the folk in the realm.

But that is another story.

ABOUT THE AUTHOR

Martin Treanor is an author and illustrator—which didn't really need saying, because he writes and illustrates all the Trumplethinskin books. He likes coffee, cake, and cake—doesn't live anywhere snazzy but he did write two other cool books: *The Silver Mist* and *Dark Creed*. He also wrote a load of short stories too . . . oh, and illustrated some other stuff.
He likes cake.

More at: *www.MartinTreanor.com*
Martin Treanor is represented by
DRPZ™ [www.drpz.net]

Look for our thin-skinned "hero" in
Trumplethinskin in the Land of UcK and
Trumplethinskin and the Gigantic Peach!

For more information about this Very Stable Genius, please visit:

TheTalesOfTrumplethinskin.com
MartinTreanor.com
ANiceCuppaTea.com

@TrumpleTales

TINY HANDS PRESS

RATCATCHERS
Ye Olde Dating Service for Fickle Folk

NAME: Trumplethinskin
OCCUPATION: Make-believer and accumulator of magic beans
LIKES: Magic beans
DISLIKES: Fake news and not having my own throne
BEST QUALITY: Stable genius
WORST QUALITY: None—I am best at everything
FAVORITE FOOD: Beautiful chocolate cake
FAVORITE THING: My golden toilet

PROFILE:

I am not a catch, but what does that matter . . . eh?
I live in *Not Far Far Away Enough* and will, one day, be king of the world (well, a stable genius like me has to have aspirations). I own a golden toilet that I sit on regularly, have a lovely roly-poly belly, and a beautiful orange face.
Get with me and I'll show you the best three seconds of your life.
No elves, hobgoblins, or pixies—as I only make dodgy deals with those.

www.ingramcontent.com/pod-product-compliance
Lightning Source LLC
Chambersburg PA
CBHW042001070526
44583CB00005BA/167